Evaluating Products and Projects to Meet Corporate Objectives

Evaluating Products and Projects to Meet Corporate Objectives

Frank A. Tillman

Deandra T. Cassone

CONTENTS

ACKNOWLEDGMENTS

We would like to acknowledge C.L. Hwang for his significant contribution in this field. His books on multiple attribute decision making, multiple objective decision making and group decision making provide a compilation of decision science methods in these areas and are fundamental in establishing the field of decision science as an area of study.

We would also like to acknowledge our family and friends who continue to support us in our efforts.

INTRODUCTION

The goal of this book is to walk individuals through a process which can be used to evaluate products or projects within your organization. The approach described in the book has been used in numerous consulting engagements with Fortune 500 companies, the military and government agencies and has provided those organizations with a sound, decision-science based approach to evaluating projects and products in their company.

The book provides an overview of the science associated with the process and step-by-step templates that can be used to support these processes. A more in-depth coverage of the decision science topics covered in this book and real-world examples are described in other books by the authors including "The Science of Common Sense: Best Practical Decision Science Methods," "A Professional's Guide to Decision Science and Problem Solving: An Integrated Approach for Assessing Issues, Finding Solutions, and Reaching Corporate Objectives," and other eBooks published by the Financial Times Press.

The book is divided into sections to segment the process so that you can perform the evaluation process. Chapter 1 discusses establishing goals and objectives for the organization. Chapter 2 involves the process required to develop criteria and metrics to determine how well we meet the goals and objectives. Chapter 3 discusses the group evaluation of projects and products and Chapter 4 describes the product and project evaluation process based on the techniques provided in the previous sections. The appendix is an example study performed by working professional graduate students using these processes.

The goal of this book is to provide a structured framework to evaluate projects and products so that organizational decisions contribute to the accomplishment of the goals and objectives of the organization. This robust, analytical framework provides for defensible decisions within an organization.

1.0 ESTABLISHING GOALS AND OBJECTIVES

1.1 Management Support Required to Execute the Approach

A primary goal of the process is to drive the corporate objectives into a cross-functional analysis that best solves problems for the company as a whole. To accomplish this, senior management must establish or communicate the objectives and support the overall approach so that the appropriate executives, managers, and subject matter experts also engage in the process.

Identifying the goals and objectives of the organization requires upper management involvement in setting goals and communicating these goals to the decision makers at all levels of the organization. Upper management is interviewed by facilitators to help determine a consensus of the corporate objectives. This involves discussing the corporate and departmental objectives and goals with all the business components, such as operations, sales, marketing and finance.

To understand the problem, you must understand the decisions that must be made at each level. This includes defining the questions so that the answers are consistent with the corporate and individual goals. The answers to the following questions should support overall corporate goals.

> How much should I produce of a product in each of the product lines?
>
> What research items should be funded?
>
> What are my warehousing requirements?
>
> How does my production affect my inventory requirements?
>
> What should I plan to produce to meet customer demand?
>
> How can I optimize scheduling delivery vehicles?
>
> And, many others.

You must also determine what you can actually change and what you cannot change within the organization. For example, if an organization wants to determine products to keep in a product line, it is not likely that the flagship items should be removed from the product line without considering their impact on all products.

Fixed operating constraints that you cannot change may also exist. This may include any number of constraints on current operations such as plant capacities, warehouse space, and the amount of resources available for spending in a given year. Usually a whole range of operating constraints exists from manufacturing, warehousing, distribution, and other areas of the company that affect the decision latitude that can be made.

You need to define the operating constraints and the variables associated with the actual decisions to be made, such as things that can be rationally changed in the normal course of business operations. This may include things such as plant throughput, funding of programs, sales commission structures, and others. The idea here is to determine what decisions can be made or changed and what cannot be changed. Understanding the decision limitations within an organization defines the operating constraints of the decision process.

The result of this are the definition of the objectives and then the decisions to be made and the metrics used to measure the success of the proposed decisions.

1.2 Solving the Right Problem

The process of organizational decision making is complex because executives may have their own goals independent of the corporate goals. The challenge is to balance the individual objectives and goals with the corporate objectives and goals both in the short and long term.

Traditionally, decisions are made in a stovepipe fashion. That is, each functional area makes decisions that are best for it without regard to the needs of the other functions, for example, manufacturing is not concerned with marketing or distribution or finance. The reason for this is the reward system for each functional area focuses only on the efficiency for that system. That is, the plant manager or operations manager is rewarded for such things as utilization of assets, return on assets, throughput, quality, minimum labor cost, and scrap for the units produced. None of these factors measure marketing efficiencies or any other functions. Marketing, for example, is basically measured and rewarded for total sales and not on specific products or product mix. When each function goes its separate way and decisions are made that improve that single function, who is looking out for the company as a whole? It begs the question, "Who is running the company?" Is it running by default where the strongest personality drives the company from their functional perspective? How, then, can you develop an overall plan for the good of the company where individual functions are sacrificed a little for the overall good. This may result in manufacturing making products that don't fully utilize the production assets; where marketing doesn't maximize the total volume sales but sells an optimum mix of products that maximize customer service and maximize profitability. You can then see it would be much better overall if there were a combined reward system so that the overall good of the organization is achieved in place of individual goals in the short and long term.

This leads to the issue of how best to manage the many objectives and how to tradeoff between them so that the entire organization prospers now and in the future. To do this you must first state what are the organizations goals and objectives. You must first specifically determine what these goals are in the short term and for the future and then set up metrics to measure how well you accomplished them. One way to do this is to ask some difficult questions. What are you trying accomplish within the company? What are you trying to accomplish at each organizational level? Unfortunately, most firms do not spend time asking these questions, or if they do, they don't implement the answers into their everyday operations. Why does this happen in nearly all the corporations large and small and at every level? Although everyone's intentions are good in setting corporate objectives, the major problem is that with today's approach to management, the objectives are ill-defined and consequently impossible to implement. How then can you ensure the corporate objectives are implemented throughout the organization, and how can you measure their success? The primary reason corporate objectives are not implemented at the operations level (which is the only place they can make an impact) is that they usually are subservient to individual manager's objectives. Also, once the objectives are set, they don't develop metrics that measure the degree of success in accomplishing them.

Thus you must ask, "How can we get there if we don't know where we are going?" More specifically, what are you trying to accomplish at the corporate level, at the functional level, and most important at the individual or action level? A great deal of effort goes into establishing a 5-year plan and identifying a number of corporate objectives with everyone pretending to agree, knowing full well the plan will be put on the shelf and promptly forgotten after the exercise is over. There is a much better way to develop a framework for improving operations.

1.3 Developing an Understanding of the Problem

This phase of the process is focused on developing an understanding of what the organization wants to accomplish. In this process you ask the difficult questions and correctly interpret the answers that reveal the correct problems.

Answering these questions requires getting key individuals to look closely at what they each want accomplish individually and companywide. This process takes thought and reflection by management. Starting this type of thought process makes management focus on its individual needs and then integrate them into the overall needs of the organization. Many times, individuals are not overtly aware of how solving their problems impact the other divisions within their company. Bringing these individuals together and addressing the problems forces them to look at their problems as total organizational problems.

1.4 Defining Goals and Objectives of a Company or Organization

You can use a number of different methods and approaches to define corporate goals and objectives, using formal and informal procedures. Doing this can provide the organization with a definition of its goals and objectives that represent its current thinking. These goals and objectives can then be integrated into the decision-making process so that decisions made with the decision model are structured to impact all levels of the organization and are quantifiable and defensible.

In establishing corporate goals and objectives, consider using management to get a group consensus. Available group decision-making techniques vary in degrees of formality and you can use them to facilitate this process. Techniques range from simple brainstorming to more sophisticated methods. The end result should be a clear definition of what a corporation views as its goals and objectives. When defined, these goals and objectives can then be built into the decision process. Following is a sequence of steps that you can use to establish the goals and objectives of an organization.

1.4.1 Establish Goals and Objectives

The first step involves establishing the objectives for the organization. Primary decision makers should meet together to ensure that all the components of the organization are represented in the decision process and are represented in the objectives. One approach is to provide to the group a "straw man" list of corporate objectives as a starting point in the development of the final list of objectives. The straw man list is based on the objectives that have historically been deemed important to the group and may include objectives such as maximizing profitability, minimizing risk, minimizing cost, or maximizing growth. The management group can then use these as a starting point and brainstorm to add or delete from the list. As part of this process, the group should also provide a high-level definition of the objectives so that all involved understand what is meant by them.

Another method, the Nominal Group Technique (NGT), which utilizes a written form for the generation of ideas, is a more formalized method that you can use to develop corporate objectives. This method attempts to minimize conforming influences and maintain social-emotional relationships in the process. It provides for equality of participation and for all members to influence the group decision through voting and ordering of priorities. "The Science of Common Sense: Best Practical Decision Science Methods," Tillman and Cassone (2015) provides a description of this process.

Managers may not have the authority to affect high-level decisions, however, the establishment of these objectives and the development of the subsequent decision criteria and metrics give managers a defensible position in their decisions. The objectives established in this manner can provide the building blocks for establishing the decision criteria and metrics used within the decision model.

It is also beneficial to establish a mission statement for the organization. A mission statement is a succinct statement, typically one sentence that summarizes the purpose of the organization. A mission statement describes why the organization is in business and what it wants to accomplish.

When any group of individuals meet to conduct activities such as this, it is difficult to arrive at complete agreement. You need to understand upfront that this may be the case. In this process, you must leave the latitude to "agree to disagree." That is, it is okay if there is not a complete agreement on all the objectives. Not all objectives may have the same importance to each function of an organization. Weighting the objectives, as described in the next section, provides a means to address that not all individuals may feel the same about the importance of each objective, which can be handled in the modeling process.

Examples of corporate objectives by different industries are shown here.

Service companies

Improve contract performance.

Minimize operating costs.

Improve customer management.

Manufacturing companies

    Minimize manufacturing costs.

    Maximize customer service.

    Minimize distribution costs.

Distribution companies

    Minimize operating costs.

    Reduce inventory levels.

    Improve operating cycle time.

Insurance companies

    Maximize customer service.

    Streamline information technology.

    Improve service delivery margin.

Food Industry companies

    Improve profitability.

    Increase market share.

    Increase sales.

    Reduce manufacturing costs.

    Reduce distribution costs.

These objectives are broad in nature and can focus management on organizational-level goals. Objectives are weighted to further focus corporate management on key operating areas within the company. Specific decision criteria and metrics further refine the key attributes that constitute the corporate measurement of the objectives. The objectives provide the starting point for the decomposition of strategic goals into actionable activities and problem solving.

Example: A company would like to use this process to provide a clearer strategic direction to the activities of the company and align their resource investment in products and projects with their corporate objectives. The company has indicated three corporate objectives shown below.

- Improve financial position
- Enhance technology development
- Improve market position

Table 1.1 shows the corporate goals and provides a high-level definition of these metrics.

Table 1.1 Example of Goals and Objectives for a Company

Objectives	Definitions
Improve Financial Position	Improve the financial position by evaluating the project or product's financial contribution to the company.
Enhance Technology Development	Improve the technological position by evaluating the project or product's ability to meet the technology development and innovation needs of the company and customers.
Improve Market Position	Improve the market position of the company with this product or project.

Brainstorm a number of corporate goals and objectives as a group. Develop a consensus of the objectives. You may agree to disagree or may easily develop this list. Write down the top objectives and provide a definition for that objective. Table 1.2 provides a template for Developing Corporate Goals and Objectives.

Table 1.2 Template for Developing Corporate Goals and Objectives

Corporate Goals and Objectives	Definition

1.4.2 Weight the Objectives to Determine Their Importance

Many times goals and objectives can be stated as being important to an organization but the relative importance of them is not quantified. In addition, there are typically conflicting objectives in which the improvement in one area may adversely impact another area. For example, improvements in information technology may also lead to increases in capital costs.

This step involves generating an overall importance for each of the established goals and objectives. This is accomplished by having each of the team members weigh the objectives established in the previous step for their view of overall importance in decisions. You can simply average the weights provided by the individuals on the team or can use other decision science methods discussed in "The Science of Common Sense: Best Practical Decision Science Methods," Tillman and Cassone (2015).

Table 1.3 Example Goal Weighting

Weights	Objectives	Definitions
40%	Improve Financial Position	Improve the financial position by evaluating the project or product's financial contribution to the company.
20%	Enhance Technology Development	Improve the technological position by evaluating the project or product's ability to meet the technology development and innovation needs of the company and customers.
40%	Improve Market Position	Improve the market position of the company with this product or project.

Assign your view of importance of each of the goals allocating a portion of 100% to each of the goals. Ensure that your total weighting of all goals sums to 100%. Table 1.4 is provided as a template to develop the importance weighting of the goals and objectives.

Table 1.4 Assign Importance Weighting to Corporate Goals and Objectives

Corporate Goals and Objectives	Definition	Importance Weighting

1.4.3 Experts Judgment/Group Participation

The problem of group decision making can be broadly classified into two categories in this field: expert judgment and group consensus. The expert judgment process entails making a decision by using experts and their expertise gained through experience. Specifically, it is concerned with making judgments and constructing new solutions to the problem. On the other hand, the group consensus process involves groups that have common interests, such as executive boards and organizations, making a decision.

Expert judgment and group consensus methods involve methods commonly utilized in the group decision-making process. Creative methods used to extract, generate, and stimulate new ideas may include brainstorming, brainwriting or Nominal Group technique. Techniques that are used to explore and clarify existing issues might include surveys, conferences, and the SPAN technique. Table 1.5 shows an example of the consensus weighting.

Table 1.5 Example of Consensus Weighting for Objectives

Objectives	Member 1	Member 2	Member 3	Member 4	Member 5	Consensus
Improve Financial Position	40%	50%	40%	60%	30%	44%
Enhance Technology Development	30%	20%	50%	30%	40%	34%
Improve Market Position	30%	30%	10%	10%	30%	22%

Each team member assigns their weighting for the corporate goals and objectives. Assign weights between 0% and 100%. The sum of the weights should equal to 100%. Average the weights across all members to develop a group consensus weighting for the objectives. Use Table 1.6 below as a template to assist in the process.

This weighting scheme can also be generated by the Normalized Direct Weighting scheme where each team member assigns a score on a scale from 1 to 10, where 10 was the most important. These can then be averaged to determine a group weighting of the objectives. These then are totaled and normalized for the individuals and the group overall.

Table 1.6 Template for Group Consensus Weighting of Objectives

Objectives	Member 1	Member 2	Member 3	Member 4	Member 5	Consensus

Objective weighting can come from senior management's view of corporate strategic direction. Another approach to weighting objectives is to determine the percent of budget that falls within a given corporate functional area. Weighting objectives using the number of dollars quantifies the magnitude of financial importance associated with a functional area. This provides a view of the potential impacts of improvement opportunities for a given functional area.

Assigning an overall importance weighting to the objectives gives the decision makers an idea of what the group as a whole views as the importance of the objectives for the organization. These objectives and their importance also provide the necessary direction and focus in the decision modeling process. You now have a better idea of what you can accomplish as an organization.

2.0 DEVELOPING DECISION CRITERIA AND METRICS TO MEET THE GOALS AND OBJECTIVES

2.1 Defining the Framework for the Decisions Being Made

You need to know what the organization wants to accomplish, the purpose of the decisions being made, and the operating environment of the organization. You can then develop the evaluation process to reflect the conditions and characteristics of the organization. Use the following question to aid in defining the framework for the model.

- What specific decisions need to be made?
- What is the business environment and constraints in which decisions are made?
- What are the firm constraints within which to achieve the goals and objectives?
- What is the flexibility of the decision to be made to achieve the goals?

Use various fact-finding efforts to answer these questions. Depending on the breadth of the evaluation, this may require that you conduct interviews with individuals in various departments and levels within the organization. Individuals currently responsible for the decisions and individuals that have been previously responsible for the decisions are good starting points to gain information. At this point in the development, this should still only be general information that you can use to outline the model being developed.

Decisions that are made with the evaluation process would dictate how the model is structured. Some examples of decisions might include the following:

- Establish budgets for the divisions and corporation as a whole.
- Determine which products should be in the product line.
- List the warehouse requirements.
- Compile the least-cost production scheduling options.
- Assess the facility conditions.
- Examine the personnel management and number and skill mix of employees.

Part of answering these questions and the nature of the information gathered in the modeling process may provide additional information that you can use to make decisions. This can also provide an opportunity to standardize the submission format of budget requests and potentially do various database queries on the submitted budget data to determine how well you make the budget.

The business environment in which the decisions are made is also important in the decision process. In an organizational environment that is dictatorial, no matter what the justification for the decision, the model may be of no use. If it is a group consensus organization, the model should reflect that type of decision-making process so that it is representative of the organization. The model should be focused forward and adaptable to changes.

To determine the framework for the model, you need to identify what elements of the operating environment are fixed and what elements of the environment can change. Fixed constraint would include those elements that have permanent limitations or restrictions in the decision process. In a production environment, it could be limitations on quantities that can be produced, steps in the manufacturing process required to create an item, warehouse limitations, and others. In budget decisions, this could involve the resource limits, limits on certain types of projects or programs funded, and others. In manpower planning, there may be limitations on the mix of skills required to perform certain activities or restrictions based on union requirements. A general overall understanding of what cannot change is as important as understanding what can be changed in the model.

Understanding the decision variables that represent the decisions to be made by the organization is equally important. Again, these variables are dependent upon the business environment of an organization and impact the type of model being built. With a model in a production environment, variables might include the amount of safety stock that is kept in-house or at remote locations or quantities of various products produced. With a model used for resource allocation, the decision may be which research and development projects you should fund.

The accuracy of the model is also an important consideration in the model development process. If a model must be accurate to a high level, such as 95 percent, the level of detail required will be much greater for a model that must be accurate to 75 percent or 80 percent. The type of data and information processing will be different for these two modeling scenarios.

Overall, Group Decision-Making techniques can be useful in many consensus-building situations within the organizational environment. These techniques are used to facilitate the establishment of corporate goals and objectives and in building decision models. Your goal here is to determine what is important to the organization and what your future direction is.

2.2 Metrics for Measuring Success

When an organization has defined and agreed upon its goals and objectives, decision makers should then develop a means to track and measure the accomplishment of these objectives. Often within an organization, a strategic plan, short-range plan, or long-range plan is developed and published as an edict to the organization. These plans may, however, end up on a shelf with no real meaning in the day-to-day operation of the organization. To drive these goals into the operating decision levels within the organization, these goals and objectives must be translated to meaningful measures of success that are used within the decision process and tracked within the organization. This is key to ensuring that the organizational goals are met. In the last section you saw how to integrate these organizational goals and weight their importance for all to follow. You now need to track their success.

Because so much data is currently available, you need to determine those measures (metrics) that provide a meaningful measure in achieving success within the organization. This process involves identifying criteria that are important to the organization. Typically decisions are made based on one or two criteria, so the metrics to support the decision process should be kept to a minimum. An approach is described in this chapter for identifying decision criteria and determining their overall importance in the decision process and measuring their success.

Based on identifying the important criteria, then data sources are assessed to determine whether this information can be relatively easily obtained, processed, and maintained. Data should be assessed to determine what level of detail should be maintained for it to be used as a metric to measure success. It may be tracked, for example, on a plant-by-plant basis or rolled up across the organization as a whole. Data can come from both automated sources or from assessments made by experienced executives or experts in the field. The process to establish, track, and maintain metrics and measures of success for an organization provides meaningful information in achieving success and understanding the organization's operations at every level.

2.3 Definition of a Metric

A metric is a standard measure to assess performance in a particular activity. A metric is a composite of measures that yield systematic insight into the state of the process or products and drives appropriate action. Metrics can be composed of both objective data such as historical data reported in a database and subjective data such as expert opinions by senior management or experts in the business.

Metrics are important for a number of reasons. You can use them to defend and justify decisions, to provide objective assessment of progress toward goals, and for problem solving and to validate process improvement. Successful enterprises constantly assess themselves and improve in all dimensions of their enterprise. Metrics provide a foundation for the assessment of success of an activity or enterprise.

A good metric is built upon an organization's missions, goals, and objectives. A metric must be meaningful and understandable for management and workers alike. The best metrics derive naturally from the process in which the data is relevant to the process and its collection becomes part of the process. The metric itself must be easily measurable. The requirement for new systems and data to implement a metric should be minimal because if not, data will not be gathered to support it.

Suppose you have established a corporate objective to improve the company's financial position. Metrics you can use to support that objective may include EBIT/EBITDA (Earnings before interest and taxes, and earnings before interest, taxes, depreciation, and amortization), FCF (Free cash flow; the sum of operating cash flow, financing cash flow, and investment cash flow), EPS (Earning per share; net earnings or profit divided by the total number of shares issued) or others. Many times, only financial metrics are considered. Projects or products may be viewed only from a Net Present Value or Return on Investment perspective. It is important to recognize that strategic, marketing, technology and other objectives are also important to the future and direction of a company. This is one of the reasons that we address a breadth of objectives and metrics in this evaluation process. Please see "A Professional's Guide to Decision Science and Problem Solving: An Integrated Approach for Assessing Issues, Finding Solutions, and Reaching Corporate Objectives," Tillman and Cassone (2012) for more information on this subject.

Key decision criteria and metrics should be limited to the critical metrics so that they are manageable and definitive goals that specific problem solving and improvement activities can be measured against. A company may choose any number of decision criteria and metrics to measure project success and evaluate the achievement of its goals. It is better, however, to measure against a few critical criteria rather than try to measure against interrelated criteria or less critical measures.

2.4 Developing Decision Criteria and Metrics

This approach to metrics development has been used in many private sector and government evaluations. The approach is to relate metrics directly to the accomplishment of the goals and objectives of the organization. This process requires the management team to critically examine goals and objectives to ensure the decisions directly relate to these objectives. Decision makers must first establish the goals and objectives and their relative importance in the final decision process. The development of goals and objectives is mentioned in the previous section.

Decision criteria and metrics are then established to support these established goals and objectives. Group decision-making techniques are also utilized to provide a means for developing the decision criteria and weighting their importance. All the decision makers should have a say in the final selection decision to ensure objectivity and avoid having dominant personalities overly control the process. The steps involved in this time-tested approach follows:

Step 1   Establish overall objectives and goals. (Chapter 1)

Step 2   Weight the objectives to determine their importance. (Chapter 1)

Step 3   Select the decision criteria.

Step 4   Weight the criteria to determine their importance.

Step 5   Develop metrics.

Overall, this approach provides a consistent, traceable, and defensible basis for making decisions.

2.4.1 Step 1: Establish Overall Objectives and Goals

The first step is establishing objectives and goals for an organization. Goals and objectives are established, noting their common basis and required common theme to represent these objectives. These objectives are then used in the development of the preliminary metrics schema. The initial cut is continued to be refined until a final set of goals and objectives are established that satisfies the group. Group decision-making techniques are used to gain this consensus. This was accomplished in Chapter 1.

2.4.2 Step 2: Weight the Objectives to Determine Their Importance

The goals and objectives are then weighted to assess the relative importance of the selected goals and objectives. Group decision-making techniques are also utilized to facilitate this process. A resulting importance weighting scheme is then developed and reviewed with the decision makers. In each step of the process, the decision makers must understand and agree to the methodologies used in the process. This was accomplished in Chapter 1.

2.4.3 Step 3: Select the Decision Criteria

For each of the objectives established in step 1, the group must establish a hierarchy of decision criteria to represent the various objectives. Define the decision criteria so that there is a clear understanding of the criteria used and what metrics will be used to measure the criteria. This definition phase provides the framework for establishing the metrics associated with each of the decision criteria. A "first cut" of the overall decision criteria will be developed, reviewed, and revised as necessary by the decision makers and senior management. Table 2.1 shows an example of the corporate goals with their associated decision criteria.

Table 2.1 Example of Decision Criteria Supporting Corporate Objectives

Objectives	Decision Criteria
Improve Financial Position	
	Return on Resources Invested
	Impact on Operating Cost
	Net Present Value
Enhance Technology Development	
	Probability of Technological Success
	Technology Development Requirements
	Innovation
Improve Market Position	
	Market Size
	Market Growth Potential
	Market Attractiveness

Group consensus building techniques will be required to arrive at the decision criteria that support the corporate goals and objectives. It may also be difficult to narrow down those key decision criteria that support accomplishing corporate objectives. However, the discussion and understanding that is developed in this process can be very beneficial to the corporate participants and leaders. Table 2.2 provides a template for developing decision criteria. The end result will be a focused understanding of what areas of measure are important to the company's success.

Table 2.2 Template to Develop Decision Criteria Supporting Corporate Objectives

Corporate Objectives	Decision Criteria

The decision criteria should then be defined to ensure that all corporate participants have an accurate understanding of the meaning of the decision criteria. Additionally, the units of measure should be agreed upon by the group. This involves determine the type of data that will be used to evaluate the project or product (subjective data, objective data) and any scaling associated with the data in the analysis. This provides a clear framework for evaluation for the corporate participants.

Table 2.3 shows an example of the decision criteria definitions that support corporate objectives. Table 2.4 provides a template to develop decision criteria, their definitions and their metrics to support your evaluation process.

Table 2.3 Example of Decision Criteria Supporting Corporate Objectives

Objectives	Decision Criteria	Definitions	Objective or Subjective Data for Metrics
Improve Financial Position		Improve the financial position by evaluating the project or product's financial contribution to the company.	
	Return on Resources Invested	Projected return on the resources invested in the product or project.	Objective
	Impact on Operating Cost	An assessment of how this product or project will impact operating costs. Scaled assessment of negative impact (increase), neutral or positive impact (reduce).	Subjective
	Net Present Value	The Net Present Value of the product or project using the company's discount rate.	Objective
Enhance Technology Development		Improve the technological position by evaluating the project or product's ability to meet the technology development and innovation needs of the company and customers.	
	Probability of Technological Success	An assessment of the probability of the successful development of this technology.	Subjective
	Technology Development Requirements	An assessment of whether the development of this technology requires new products or processes or whether it can be accomplished with currently available capital assets or technologies	Subjective
	Innovation	Is this an innovative technology, enhancement to current technology or are similar to currently available technologies.	Subjective
Improve Market Position		Improve the market position of the company with this product or project.	
	Market Size	The projected market size of this product or project.	Subjective
	Market Growth Potential	The potential impact that this product or project has on market growth.	Subjective
	Market Attractiveness	The market attractiveness of this product or project. This is a subjective assessment but should be based on market research.	Subjective

Table 2.4 Template for the Development of Decision Criteria and Metrics

Objectives	Decision Criteria	Definitions	Objective or Subjective Data for Metrics

2.4.4 Step 4: Weight the Criteria to Determine Their Importance

Team members then weight the criteria established in step 3 for their relative importance in the decision process. Again, use group decision-making techniques to facilitate this process. The team must develop a "first cut" of the decision criteria weights and review and revise their findings to ensure reasonableness.

Table 2.5 shows an example of the decision criteria weighting for each of the team members. Their importance score is then averaged as a consensus weighting for the group.

Table 2.5 Example of Consensus Weighting for Decision Criteria

Objectives	Decision Criteria	Member 1	Member 2	Member 3	Member 4	Member 5	Consensus
Improve Financial Position							
	Return on Resources Invested	30%	20%	25%	40%	15%	26%
	Impact on Operating Cost	40%	60%	40%	30%	35%	41%
	Net Present Value	30%	20%	35%	30%	50%	33%
Enhance Technology Development							
	Probability of Technological Success	45%	30%	35%	45%	40%	39%
	Technology Development Requirements	30%	40%	25%	25%	35%	31%
	Innovation	25%	30%	40%	30%	25%	30%
Improve Market Position							
	Market Size	20%	30%	35%	40%	35%	32%
	Market Growth Potential	50%	25%	35%	30%	35%	35%
	Market Attractiveness	30%	45%	30%	30%	30%	33%

Table 2.6 provides a template to develop decision criteria weighting for team members.

Table 2.6 Template for Consensus Weighting for Decision Criteria

Objectives	Decision Criteria	Member 1	Member 2	Member 3	Member 4	Member 5	Consensus

Table 2.7 shows an example of the weights resulting from the consensus objective weights and the corporate decision criteria weights. The resulting criteria weights show how important the team members as a whole viewed each of the individual decision criteria. This information will be used further in our evaluation process.

Table 2.7 Example of Weights Resulting from the Objective and Decision Criteria Consensus Weighting.

Objective Weights	Objectives	Decision Criteria Weights	Decision Criteria	Resulting Weight
40%	Improve Financial Position			
		26%	Return on Resources Invested	10%
		41%	Impact on Operating Cost	16%
		33%	Net Present Value	13%
20%	Enhance Technology Development			
		39%	Probability of Technological Success	8%
		31%	Technology Development Requirements	6%
		30%	Innovation	6%
40%	Improve Market Position			
		32%	Market Size	13%
		35%	Market Growth Potential	14%
		33%	Market Attractiveness	13%

Table 2.8 provides a template to generate resulting criteria weights based on the consensus building activities.

Table 2.8 Template for Weights Resulting from the Objective and Decision Criteria Consensus Weighting.

Corporate Objectives	Objective Weights	Decision Criteria and Metrics	Decision Criteria Weights	Resulting Criteria Weights

2.4.5 Step 5: Develop Decision Criteria Metrics

From the decision criteria established in step 3, you can identify the metrics. This involves determining what data to use to measure and quantify the decision criteria. The criteria can be either subjective or quantitative in nature. You can measure criteria using "hard," quantitative data or a subjective scale of the decision makers. Expert opinion can be subjectively used when objective data is not available or when objective data is too costly or time-consuming to obtain. Again, the group must develop a "first cut" of the decision criteria metrics and review and revise its findings as needed to satisfy the decision makers. Table 2.9 shows an example of decision criteria and whether these criteria will be quantified with objective or subjective measures and the measures to be used in the evaluation. Table 2.10 provides a template to develop the metrics for the decision criteria.

Table 2.9 Example of Decision Criteria Definitions and Metrics

Objectives	Decision Criteria	Definitions	Objective or Subjective Data for Metrics
Improve Financial Position		Improve the financial position by evaluating the project or product's financial contribution to the company.	
	Return on Resources Invested	Projected return on the resources invested in the product or project.	Objective - Percentage
	Impact on Operating Cost	An assessment of how this product or project will impact operating costs. Scaled assessment of negative impact (increase) , neutral or positive impact (reduce).	Subjective - Based on projected operating costs
	Net Present Value	The Net Present Value of the product or project using the company's discount rate.	Objective - Dollars
Enhance Technology Development		Improve the technological position by evaluating the project or product's ability to meet the technology development and innovation needs of the company and customers.	
	Probability of Technological Success	An assessment of the probability of the successful development of this technology.	Subjective - Percentage
	Technology Development Requirements	An assessment of whether the development of this technology requires new products or processes or whether it can be accomplished with currently available capital assets or technologies	Subjective - Subjective scale addressing the ability to leverage existing technology or the requirement = 5 to develop new resources to support = 1.
	Innovation	Is this an innovative technology, enhancement to current technology or are similar to currently available technologies.	Subjective - Subjective scale where technology is innovative = 5 or similar to available technologies = 1.
Improve Market Position		Improve the market position of the company with this product or project.	
	Market Size	The projected market size of this product or project.	Subjective - Scaled from Low = $5 million to High = $100 million
	Market Growth Potential	The potential impact that this product or project has on market growth.	Subjective - Scaled from Flat/Negative = 1 to >20% = 5
	Market Attractiveness	The market attractiveness of this product or project. This is a subjective assessment but should be based on market research.	Subjective - Scaled from Low = 1 to High = 5

Table 2.10 Template for the Development of Decision Criteria Definitions and Metrics

Corporate Objectives	Decision Criteria	Definition	Metrics (Objective or Subjective Criteria)

2.5 Data Used to Support Metrics

You can use either objective or subjective data to represent metrics used in the decision process. Objective data usually can be described as data that can be quantified by some measure of known commonality. This may be data such as the number of items produced, number of trucks in a location, population of a city, and so on. This data is usually available in some form in company databases and information systems. Typically, statistics such as averages and trends are generated based on a record of this objective data over some point in time. Objective or quantitative data represents a history of activities of a company that has been operating during a given time period.

Qualitative or subjective data can be easily used in a number of different situations. Surveys are good examples of subjective data used to represent a rating of a product or service. Use scales from 1 to 5 or 1 to 10 to represent high, medium, and low assessments for a given metrics. Use assessments such as red, yellow, and green in other situations in which individuals (such as military personnel) might find more meaning in rating conditions. Numerical values with their verbal description provide the type of information that can be captured and utilized in a decision model when other information is not available.

Subjective data is data based on someone's opinion or best guess of a condition or a future event. Subjective data is more qualitative in nature in that it defines a situation or condition without specific data points. Subjective data can be generated by individuals within or outside of a company or experts within a given field of operation.

Typically, subjective data or opinions provide insights into a subjective assessment of a metric. Subjective data and expert opinions are typically forward looking in nature trying to predict what will happen in the future. Individuals make assessments based on what has happened in the past and what may happen in the future. Objective data, especially in the form of statistics, however, is based on historical data, thus projecting the future , what has happened in the past, which assumes that the future will behave much like the past. The entire business environment may have changed, thus, what has happened in the past may be a poor representation of the future; thus a new source of data is required.

Following is a simple scale example that you can use to represent the assessment of the future development potential of a given market.

Future Market Potential

Definition: The projection that this market will become a substantial market in future corporate activities.

Highly Probable	5
	4
Moderately Probable	3
	2
Unlikely	1

This type of information is good information to capture from the experts and decision makers. Utilizing this type of information along with statistics fills gaps that exist to get a better representation of factors that influence future activities.

In developing goals, decision criteria, and constraints, consider a number of parameters in the development process to ensure a set of well-structured, well-represented goals and decision criteria. These development parameters are as follows:

- Goals and decision criteria must represent actual and important considerations in making decisions. Examples would include reducing logistics costs, improving call center response times, and so on.

- Decision criteria must differentiate one project from another in terms of higher or lower priority. This would involve capturing key project characteristics that differ among projects, such as impacts to different functional areas, costs, completion time, and so on.

- Decision criteria must be independent, not overlapping in content or intent, to avoid accounting for the same thought or idea more than once. This tends to overweight the importance of certain criteria. Instances may occur in which both a component cost and a total cost are considered. The component cost would overlap with the total cost value.

- Decision criteria must be defined as clearly as possible to ensure that the decision criteria in the evaluation process are viewed in the same context. Individuals have different perspectives associated with various terms and definitions. The definitions must be clear.

- Measures and scales developed for the decision criteria must be meaningful in the evaluation process and the data to perform the evaluation easily accessible. Objective data provides a basis for a relatively clear scale or measure. The use of subjective criteria requires that the scale components are clearly defined and represent a natural language intention and meaning.

- Constraints that represent types of mixes, qualifiers, and conditions that would be applied to a prioritized list of items must be identified and differentiated from the evaluation decision criteria. You must define the operating parameters. This may be total budget, capacity constraints, and manpower availability. All of these components put bounds around the issue addressed.

3.0 GROUP EVALUATION OF PROJECTS AND PRODUCTS

3.1 Introduction of Group Evaluation of Projects and Products

Chapters 1 and 2 of the book involve the establishment of objectives and goals, decision criteria, measures, weighting for the purpose of evaluating and prioritizing projects and products for an organization. The previous sections were developed to lead the team through the process to evaluate projects with the established decision criteria for a planning period. This process provides a standardized evaluation process and will enable corporate participants to use a standardized process for making decisions. Once the decision criteria, metrics and the importance weighting have been established, corporate participants can now begin to evaluate their products or projects within the established framework. This is described in a number of steps in this section.

Weighting the importance of corporate objectives and decision criteria is accomplished with group consensus weighting. This is also done when evaluating projects and products. Each individual has a voice in the evaluation process and a group evaluation is generated from these individual evaluation team project evaluations.

A model is used to provide feedback to the evaluation team on their impact of their votes on the project and project prioritization. All the decision makers had input into the decision process, which ensures objectivity in the prioritization process. The prioritization process provides the foundation for establishing an objective, structured evaluation and prioritization which provides the organization with a traceable and defensible basis for decisions. The following specific activities are involved in the completion of this effort.

3.2 Project Evaluation Process

From the information gathered from the previous steps of the example, the following process is agreed upon in the development of a model to evaluate projects and products. An execution model is built based on this process and a brief description of these steps are discussed next.

3.2.1 Communicate Goals and Decision Criteria and Their Importance Weighting for Project Evaluation to Managers

The goals and decision criteria are first re-weighted based on the finalized list of decision criteria. A group consensus weighting is generated and then communicated to the managers along with the goals and decision criteria. This communication ensures that the managers are aware of the criteria and their importance so they can adequately address these issues in their briefing packets.

Table 2.7 is reprinted as Table 3.1 to display the objective and decision criteria weights and will be used in our example.

Table 3.1 Goal and Decision Criteria Weights

Objective Weights	Objectives	Decision Criteria Weights	Decision Criteria	Resulting Weight
40%	Improve Financial Position			
		26%	Return on Resources Invested	10%
		41%	Impact on Operating Cost	16%
		33%	Net Present Value	13%
20%	Enhance Technology Development			
		39%	Probability of Technological Success	8%
		31%	Technology Development Requirements	6%
		30%	Innovation	6%
40%	Improve Market Position			
		32%	Market Size	13%
		35%	Market Growth Potential	14%
		33%	Market Attractiveness	13%

3.2.2 Managers Submit/Present Packages to the Evaluation Team

The managers brief the evaluation team with the projects and provide briefing packets to the evaluation team as required. The briefing package is industry and company specific, but is used to provide additional information to the decision makers. Companies will have different formats for this type of presentation or may not require a product to be presented for evaluation.

3.2.3 Evaluation Team Evaluates Projects Based on Established Goals and Decision Criteria

Each evaluation team member evaluates, via an evaluation form, the projects and products with the established goals and decision criteria. Table 3.2 shows an example of an evaluation form that could be used to assess projects or products under consideration.

Table 3.2 Example Project/Product Evaluation

Project or Product Name:	New Product One
Description:	This is a new technology to support our core operations.
Sponsor/Funding Agency:	Product Development
Budget:	$500,000
Time to Complete:	6 months

Decision Criteria	Definitions	Objective or Subjective Data for Metrics	Member 1 Evaluation
Goal 1: Improve Financial Position	Improve the financial position by evaluating the project or product's financial contribution to the company.		
Return on Resources Invested	Projected return on the resources invested in the product or project.	Objective - Percentage	25%
Impact on Operating Cost	An assessment of how this product or project will impact operating costs. Scaled assessment of negative impact (increase) , neutral or positive impact (reduce).	Subjective - Based on projected operating costs Scale 1=Low to 5 = High	3
Net Present Value	The Net Present Value of the product or project using the company's discount rate.	Objective - Dollars	$3,500,000
Goal 2: Enhance Technology Development	Improve the technological position by evaluating the project or product's ability to meet the technology development and innovation needs of the company and customers.		
Probability of Technological Success	An assessment of the probability of the successful development of this technology.	Subjective - Percentage	80%
Technology Development Requirements	An assessment of whether the development of this technology requires new products or processes or whether it can be accomplished with currently available capital assets or technologies	Subjective - Subjective scale addressing the ability to leverage existing technology or the requirement = 5 to develop new resources to support = 1.	4
Innovation	Is this an innovative technology, enhancement to current technology or are similar to currently available technologies.	Subjective - Subjective scale where technology is innovative = 5 or similar to available technologies = 1.	3

Decision Criteria	Definitions	Objective or Subjective Data for Metrics	Member 1 Evaluation
Goal 3: Improve Market Position	Improve the market position of the company with this product or project.		
Market Size	The projected market size of this product or project.	Subjective - Scaled from Low = 1 ($5 million) to High = 5 ($100 million)	4
Market Growth Potential	The potential impact that this product or project has on market growth.	Subjective - Scaled from Flat/Negative = 1 to >20% = 5	4
Market Attractiveness	The market attractiveness of this product or project. This is a subjective assessment but should be based on market research.	Subjective - Scaled from Low = 1 to High = 5	3

Table 3.3 is a template that can be used to develop the product or project evaluation process. This type of evaluation form would be customized for individual companies and different types of evaluations.

Table 3.3 Project/Product Evaluation Template

Project or Product Name:
Description:
Sponsor/Funding Agency:
Budget:
Time to Complete:

Decision Criteria	Definitions	Objective or Subjective Data for Metrics	Member 1 Evaluation
Goal 1:			
Goal 2:			
Goal 3:			

Evaluations are combined (averaged) for the group to determine an overall project evaluation. A combination or group consensus evaluation process enables all decision makers to have a voice in the evaluation process. Some data is objective, therefore won't change from member-to-member. However, when the data is subjective, different members or decision makers could have substantially different views on the merit of the product or project. Using a consensus evaluation approach captures these differences.

It should also be noted that the evaluation process offers a means to define, explore and evaluate the different views of the members. One group member may have a significantly different background or type of expertise, and discussing the differences will provide insights to the other members of the group and to the decision overall.

Additionally, this evaluation and discussion process may require a re-evaluation of the products or projects or may also expose certain circumstances where the evaluation measure or decision criteria need to be adjusted to better reflect the goals of the company. Understanding that this may take place and allowing for this is important. The overarching goal of this process is to capture the decision maker evaluations and better understand the product or projects being performed or launched by the company within the context of company goals.

Table 3.4 provides a summary of the group evaluations for the first product.

Table 3.4 New Product One Group Consensus Evaluation

Project or Product Name:	New Product One
Description:	This is a new technology to support our core operations.
Sponsor/Funding Agency:	Product Development
Budget:	$500,000
Time to Complete:	6 months

Objectives	Decision Criteria	Member 1	Member 2	Member 3	Member 4	Member 5	Consensus
Improve Financial Position							
	Return on Resources Invested	25%	25%	25%	25%	25%	25%
	Impact on Operating Cost	3	2	3	2	4	2.8
	Net Present Value	$3,500,000	$3,500,000	$3,500,000	$3,500,000	$3,500,000	$3,500,000
Enhance Technology Development							
	Probability of Technological Success	80%	50%	75%	70%	85%	72%
	Technology Development Requirements	4	5	2	3	2	3.2
	Innovation	3	2	2	2	2	2.2
Improve Market Position							
	Market Size	4	4	4	3	5	4
	Market Growth Potential	4	5	2	5	5	4.2
	Market Attractiveness	3	5	4	4	2	3.6

Table 3.5 provides a template for the group consensus evaluation process.

Table 3.5 Group Consensus Evaluation Process Template

Project or Product Name:
Description:
Sponsor/Funding Agency:
Budget:
Time to Complete:

Objectives	Decision Criteria	Member 1	Member 2	Member 3	Member 4	Member 5	Consensus
Goal 1							
Goal 2							
Goal 3							

Each group member then evaluates each product and a group consensus evaluation is generated for each of the products or projects. Table 3.6 show an example of the consensus evaluation for all of the products.

Table 3.6 Group Consensus for All Product or Project Evaluations

Objectives	Improve Financial Position			Enhance Technology Development			Improve Market Position		
Decision Criteria	Return on Resources Invested	Impact on Operating Cost	Net Present Value	Probability of Technological Success	Technology Development Requirements	Innovation	Market Size	Market Growth Potential	Market Attractiveness
New Product One	25%	2.8	$3,500,000	72%	3.2	2.2	4	4.2	3.6
New Product Two	22%	3.8	$5,000,000	93%	2.9	2.4	2.4	3.4	2.8
New Product Three	35%	2.7	$1,650,000	41%	3	1.8	3.1	2.5	1.5
New Product Four	25%	2.3	$2,420,000	73%	2.8	3.8	4.5	4	3.9
New Product Five	25%	3.1	$1,800,000	48%	1.6	4	3.3	4.3	1.8
New Product Six	19%	2.1	$4,500,000	62%	2.7	2.4	3.1	1.6	2.9
New Product Seven	22%	1.6	$1,950,000	79%	1.5	2.2	1.7	1.6	3.6
New Product Eight	35%	4.3	$840,000	73%	4.5	3.7	2.3	2.5	2.1
New Product Nine	40%	4.5	$5,000,000	69%	1.7	4.1	2.9	4.3	2.1
New Product Ten	26%	4.2	$250,000	59%	3.6	1.7	2.6	3.4	1.5

4.0 PRODUCT AND PROJECT EVALUATION

4.1 Product and Project Evaluation

At this point, we have spent a significant amount of time and effort developing a framework for evaluating projects and products. The process involved in establishing corporate objectives, decision criteria and evaluation metrics has been used to establish, from a team perspective, those area that are important to the company and how we can evaluate the projects that we perform or the products that we launch so that they are aligned with where we are going as a company. The time establishing this framework provides a clear picture of how to move forward with decisions that we make as a company.

The evaluation framework that we've developed to this point has provided some insight and understanding into the product and projects that we intend to do. Not only do we have a framework for evaluation, but we are looking at each product and project carefully to see how the important contributions of it stand on its own and we can also use these evaluations to see how each of the products and projects stack up against each other.

Questions we may ask in regards to the product or project on a standalone basis include:

- Is this a viable option for the company to pursue?
- How varied were the evaluations by the team members?
- Are there aspects of the project or product that need further discussion?
- Should more development or of the scope be done for the project or product?
- Have strong individuals biased the evaluation process?

The end goal of developing a detailed evaluation process is to make the best decisions possible with the limited resources of the company. This will support the long-term strategy of the company.

Along with the individual evaluations, products and projects should be assessed against each other. There are a number of methods and approaches that can be used to support this evaluation process, but the simplest and easiest to use methods are discussed in the remaining part of this chapter.

4.2 Generate Project or Product Ranking Based on the Team Weighting of Goals and Decision Criteria and the Group Consensus Evaluations

The goals and decision criteria weighting and project evaluations are the basis for generating a product or project ranking. The scores from the evaluations are normalized for each project for each individual decision criteria. The weighting factors are then applied (multiplied) to the normalized project evaluation scores for each project and these scores are then summed across each decision criteria to generate a score for each project. Projects are then ordered from high to low in rank.

Numerous methods and algorithms exist that can be used to prioritize projects. A multiple criteria decision making technique, such as Simple Additive Weight or the Technique for Order Preference of the Similarity to the Ideal Solution (TOPSIS) can easily be used to prioritize the projects or processes. These methods are described in "The Science of Common Sense: Best Practical Decision Science Methods," Tillman and Cassone (2015). We will briefly describe the Simple Additive Weighting method and demonstrate its use with our example.

4.2.1 Simple Additive Weighting Method

The simple additive weighting method (SAW) is probably the best-known and widely used method of multiple attribute decision making. The decision maker assigns importance weights to each attribute, which become the coefficients of the variables. These weighted coefficients need to be normalized to standardize the scale of data.

To reflect the decision maker's marginal worth assessments within attributes, the decision maker also makes a numerical scaling of intra-attribute values.

The decision maker can then obtain a total score for each alternative simply by multiplying the scale rating for each attribute value by the importance weight assigned to the attribute and summing these products over all attributes. After the total scores are computed for each alternative, the alternative with the highest score (the highest weighted average) is the one suggested to the decision maker.

Important precautions when developing decision models are below.

- Scaling: Scaling of criteria value can greatly influence the impact of single criteria and thus the ranking. To avoid this problem, all values within a criterion are normalized.

- Independence: Care should be taken so that all the criteria are independent, thus avoiding overweighing the effects of a single criterion.

A global (total) score in the SAW is obtained by adding contributions from each attribute. A common numerical scaling system such as normalization (instead of single dimensional value functions) is required to permit addition among attribute values.

For each of the attributes, the scores for the decision criteria are either maximized (a bigger value is a better value) or minimized (a smaller value is a better value). This is taken into account when the decision matrix is normalized. The "best" minimum value or maximum value is identified and used as the basis for the normalization.

This is shown in the formulas below.

Minimized Attribute = $\min(x_{ij})/x_{ij}$

Maximized Attribute = $x_{ij}/\max(x_{ij})$

where $i = 1, 2, \ldots, m$ alternatives and $j = 1, 2, \ldots, n$ attributes

The following section demonstrates this with the example used in the book.

4.2.2 Product and Project Evaluation Ranking Example

Table 3.6 is used as the basis of this example. Table 4.1 shows this table and also identifies whether the decision criteria is Minimized (smaller is a better number) or Maximized (bigger is a better number). Additionally the "best score" for each of the decision criteria is identified at the bottom of the table.

Table 4.1 Product Evaluation Table

Objectives	Improve Financial Position			Enhance Technology Development			Improve Market Position		
	Maximize	Minimize	Maximize	Maximize	Maximize	Maximize	Maximize	Maximize	Maximize
Decision Criteria	Return on Resources Invested	Impact on Operating Cost	Net Present Value	Probability of Technological Success	Technology Development Requirements	Innovation	Market Size	Market Growth Potential	Market Attractiveness
New Product One	25%	2.8	$3,500,000	72%	3.2	2.2	4	4.2	3.6
New Product Two	22%	3.8	$5,000,000	93%	2.9	2.4	2.4	3.4	2.8
New Product Three	35%	2.7	$1,650,000	41%	3	1.8	3.1	2.5	1.5
New Product Four	25%	2.3	$2,420,000	73%	2.8	3.8	4.5	4	3.9
New Product Five	25%	3.1	$1,800,000	48%	1.6	4	3.3	4.3	1.8
New Product Six	19%	2.1	$4,500,000	62%	2.7	2.4	3.1	1.6	2.9
New Product Seven	22%	1.6	$1,950,000	79%	1.5	2.2	1.7	1.6	3.6
New Product Eight	35%	4.3	$840,000	73%	4.5	3.7	2.3	2.5	2.1
New Product Nine	40%	4.5	$5,000,000	69%	1.7	4.1	2.9	4.3	2.1
New Product Ten	26%	4.2	$250,000	59%	3.6	1.7	2.6	3.4	1.5
Best Score	**40%**	**1.6**	**$5,000,000**	**93%**	**4.5**	**4.1**	**4.5**	**4.3**	**3.9**

To develop a ranked list of products, the scores for each attribute must first be normalized. This will provide dimensionless units so that an overall score for each product can be generated and evaluated. Table 4.2 shows an example of the normalized product evaluation table.

Table 4.2 Normalized Product Evaluation Table.

Objectives	Improve Financial Position			Enhance Technology Development			Improve Market Position		
	Maximize	Minimize	Maximize	Maximize	Maximize	Maximize	Maximize	Maximize	Maximize
Decision Criteria	Return on Resources Invested	Impact on Operating Cost	Net Present Value	Probability of Technological Success	Technology Development Requirements	Innovation	Market Size	Market Growth Potential	Market Attractiveness
New Product One	0.625	0.571	0.700	0.774	0.711	0.537	0.889	0.977	0.923
New Product Two	0.550	0.421	1.000	1.000	0.644	0.585	0.533	0.791	0.718
New Product Three	0.875	0.593	0.330	0.441	0.667	0.439	0.689	0.581	0.385
New Product Four	0.625	0.696	0.484	0.785	0.622	0.927	1.000	0.930	1.000
New Product Five	0.625	0.516	0.360	0.516	0.356	0.976	0.733	1.000	0.462
New Product Six	0.475	0.762	0.900	0.667	0.600	0.585	0.689	0.372	0.744
New Product Seven	0.550	1.000	0.390	0.849	0.333	0.537	0.378	0.372	0.923
New Product Eight	0.875	0.372	0.168	0.785	1.000	0.902	0.511	0.581	0.538
New Product Nine	1.000	0.356	1.000	0.742	0.378	1.000	0.644	1.000	0.538
New Product Ten	0.650	0.381	0.050	0.634	0.800	0.415	0.578	0.791	0.385

The objective and decision criteria weights that were developed in Chapter 2 (Table 2.7) are now brought back into the product and project evaluation process. The group consensus weights and the group consensus decision criteria evaluations, in their normalized form, are now used to develop an overall score for each of the products. The decision criteria weights are multiplied by the normalized group consensus scores and they are summed across each project or product. The results are shown in Table 4.3 where bigger is better.

Table 4.3 Product Evaluation Score

	Normalized Weights									
	10%	16%	13%	8%	6%	6%	13%	14%	13%	
Decision Criteria	Return on Resources Invested	Impact on Operating Cost	Net Present Value	Probability of Technological Success	Technology Development Requirements	Innovation	Market Size	Market Growth Potential	Market Attractiveness	Score
New Product One	0.065	0.094	0.092	0.060	0.044	0.032	0.114	0.137	0.122	0.760
New Product Two	0.057	0.069	0.132	0.078	0.040	0.035	0.068	0.111	0.095	0.685
New Product Three	0.091	0.097	0.044	0.034	0.041	0.026	0.088	0.081	0.051	0.554
New Product Four	0.065	0.114	0.064	0.061	0.039	0.056	0.128	0.130	0.132	0.789
New Product Five	0.065	0.085	0.048	0.040	0.022	0.059	0.094	0.140	0.061	0.613
New Product Six	0.049	0.125	0.119	0.052	0.037	0.035	0.088	0.052	0.098	0.656
New Product Seven	0.057	0.164	0.051	0.066	0.021	0.032	0.048	0.052	0.122	0.614
New Product Eight	0.091	0.061	0.022	0.061	0.062	0.054	0.065	0.081	0.071	0.569
New Product Nine	0.104	0.058	0.132	0.058	0.023	0.060	0.082	0.140	0.071	0.729
New Product Ten	0.068	0.062	0.007	0.049	0.050	0.025	0.074	0.111	0.051	0.496

These scores are then used to generate an overall ranking for each of the products. These results are in Table 4.4

Table 4.4 Overall Product Ranking

Product	Score	Rank
New Product Four	0.789	1
New Product One	0.760	2
New Product Nine	0.729	3
New Product Two	0.685	4
New Product Six	0.656	5
New Product Seven	0.614	6
New Product Five	0.613	7
New Product Eight	0.569	8
New Product Three	0.554	9
New Product Ten	0.496	10

This stack ranking of products should be further explored which will be discussed in the following section on sensitivity analysis. This ranked list, however, can be used for a variety of decisions. Which include:

- Resource allocation decisions
- Budgeting decisions
- Personnel assignment decisions
- And introducing products into a product line

The following section will also discuss the use of this information in budgeting decisions.

4.3 Perform Sensitivity Analysis

Product or project evaluations can be used to make funding or resource allocation decisions. When they are used in this process, the rigor described in this book is helpful to ensure that the company best utilizes their resources. Based on the product and ranking information, Table 4.5 shows the initial investment required for launching each of the products.

Table 4.5 Product Ranking and Initial Investment

Product	Score	Rank	Initial Investment
New Product Four	0.789	1	$ 400,000
New Product One	0.760	2	$ 500,000
New Product Nine	0.729	3	$ 415,000
New Product Two	0.685	4	$ 500,000
New Product Six	0.656	5	$ 450,000
New Product Seven	0.614	6	$ 162,000
New Product Five	0.613	7	$ 150,000
New Product Eight	0.569	8	$ 75,000
New Product Three	0.554	9	$ 165,000
New Product Ten	0.496	10	$ 30,000

The product evaluation process now provides a structured approach for assigning resources. Suppose that the company has $2,500,000 to invest in the current budget cycle on these products, the following products would be funded from the above list. This is shown in Table 4.6

Table 4.6 Product Funding Decisions

Product	Score	Rank	Initial Investment	Total	
New Product Four	0.789	1	$ 400,000	$ 400,000	
New Product One	0.760	2	$ 500,000	$ 900,000	
New Product Nine	0.729	3	$ 415,000	$ 1,315,000	**Funded**
New Product Two	0.685	4	$ 500,000	$ 1,815,000	
New Product Six	0.656	5	$ 450,000	$ 2,265,000	
New Product Seven	0.614	6	$ 162,000	$ 2,427,000	
New Product Five	0.613	7	$ 150,000	$ 2,577,000	
New Product Eight	0.569	8	$ 75,000	$ 2,652,000	**Unfunded**
New Product Three	0.554	9	$ 165,000	$ 2,817,000	
New Product Ten	0.496	10	$ 30,000	$ 2,847,000	

"What-if" analysis is performed on the ranking and constrained resource allocation to determine the impact of alternate funding schemes on the list of funded projects. This might include revising the weighting scheme, determining "must-have" or "must-fund" projects, and other budgeting decisions that more concisely represent project funding requirements.

The models and results provide a means to identify the key drivers associated with the assessment of product and project alternatives. You can perform sensitivity analysis on the current ranked list of alternatives to determine how much an evaluation criteria must change to move an alternative up or down in the ranked list of projects. The importance weighting of the evaluation criteria and the evaluation scores for the alternatives drive the alternative scoring in terms meeting customer and organizational goals. Sensitivity analysis is useful in identifying the key drivers of the overall value of an alternative. The specific sub-criteria evaluations for the alternatives provide the supporting detail to show why certain alternatives received the scores they did and can be used to pinpoint potential areas for improvement and additional trades.

The importance of sensitivity analysis should be mentioned at this point, as well. We view the initial solution as a starting point in decision making. The weights drive the product ranking and should not be overlooked. We have previously used group decision-making techniques to ensure that the weights are representative of the organization. Testing the different rank order of products with different attribute weights can be done as part of sensitivity analysis with the solution. Additionally, testing the modification of the individual attributes can provide decision makers with insight into how sensitive various values are to the resulting rank order. Sensitivity analysis is an important aspect of using structured methods in the decision-making process where data may be subjective.

4.4 Additional Resources

This approach has been used in numerous consulting projects. Some of those projects have been documented in publications that can be used as additional reference for implementing this approach. The appendix provides an example of this process developed by working professional graduate students, however, real-world studies are contained in the following publications.

- *A Professional's Guide to Decision Science and Problem Solving: An Integrated Approach for Assessing Issues, Finding Solutions, and Reaching Corporate Objectives* - This book discusses a start to finish methodology for solving complex business problems. Concepts presented in this book are discussed along with a number of different tools and case studies to support the methodology.

- *The Science of Common Sense: Best Practical Decision Science Methods* – This book discusses decision science methods that the authors have found useful in real-world applications. Real real-world examples of this process and decision science approaches are provided in this book.

- *Investment Strategy for Product Development in the Aerospace Industry* – This eBook provides a detailed example of the process described in this book as executed for a military research and development lab.

- *Strategic Planning and New Product Development* – This eBook provides a detailed example of this process executed for a major chemical company with their research and new product development projects. The process is demonstrated in a computer system so that it can be used on an ongoing basis.

- *The Seven Rules for Building Effective Analytical Models for Decisions* – This short eBook provides insights and lessons learned when building decision models and implementing a structured modeling approach as is described in this book.

APPENDIX A.
EXAMPLE ASSESSING LAUNCH LOCATIONS FOR THE GOOGLE DRIVERLESS CAR

This study was developed as a class assignment by industry professionals in a graduate level course in Industrial and Manufacturing System Engineering. The students that developed the project have given permission for its use. The students are Greg Stitt, Shannon Reickert, Andres Donoso and Pedro Ortiz. This final report was reproduced in its entirety.

This study in no way represents Google or any employee's opinion of decisions or the Google decision process. This study was developed for exemplary purposes only and has no relationship to real-world decisions being made by Google. Additionally, all data was derived by from the publically available references at the end of this example.

Introduction

Google began in March 1995 as a research project by Larry Page and Sergey Brin, Ph.D. students at Stanford University. Page's web crawler began exploring the web in March 1996, with Page's own Stanford home page serving as the only starting point.

From the start, Google endeavored to do more, and to do important and meaningful things. The domain Google.com was registered in September 1997, and Larry and Sergey formally incorporated their company, on September 4, 1998 at a friend's garage in Menlo Park, California.

Google asks the "What if" questions, and then works relentlessly to see if they can find the answer. Google's core products include Search, Android, Maps, Chrome, YouTube, Google Play and Gmail. Each of these products have over one billion monthly active users. Google's vision places paramount importance on creativity and innovation.

In 2015, Google established the Alphabet Holding Company which is a collection of businesses – the largest being Google. Alphabet provides an umbrella for these businesses to operate independently, and provides money for research and development projects, such as the autonomous vehicle, or Google Car.

Revenue

Google's revenue is generated through online advertising. The company generates revenues by delivering both, performance and brand advertising.

- Performance advertising creates and delivers relevant ads that users will click, leading to direct engagement with advertisers. Most of the performance advertisers pay when a user engages in their ads.
- Brand advertising helps enhance users' awareness of and affinity with advertisers' products and services, through videos, text, images, and other interactive ads that run across various devices.

Number of Employees

As of December 31, 2015, we had 61,814 full-time employees: 23,336 in research and development, 19,082 in sales and marketing, 10,944 in operations, and 8,452 in general and administrative functions.

Competitors

The company faces formidable competition in every aspect of the business. Google's adaptability to rapid change provides the company a business edge over competitors like general purpose search engines and information services, such as Yahoo, Microsoft's Bing, Yandex, Baidu, Naver, WebCrawler, and MyWebSearch.

Vertical search engines and e-commerce websites, such as Kayak (travel queries), LinkedIn (job queries), WebMD (health queries), and Amazon and eBay (e-commerce). While, some users navigate directly to online content, websites, and apps rather than go through Google.

Some users are increasingly relying on social networks, such as Facebook and Twitter, for product or service referrals, rather than seeking information through traditional search engines.

Research and Development (R&D)

Google spent in $7.1B, $9.8B, and $12.3B in 2013, 2014, and 2015 respectively in R & D. Most of it is through the engineering and technical research and associated costs, which include $1.6B, $2.2B, and $2.7B in stock based compensation.

Moonshots

Alphabet's willingness to take risks in future technology is reflected in the autonomous vehicle project. Moonshots are game changers in the marketplace, especially in technology. Moonshots are potential huge market opportunities by taking leaps in technology. Our paper will focus on this particular moonshot by conducting analysis on the autonomous vehicle project.

Background

In 2004 DARPA, the Defense Advanced Research Projects Agency (DARPA), sponsored a Grand Challenge competition for American autonomous vehicles. Congress authorized DARPA to award cash prizes to further DARPA's mission. Which is to sponsor revolutionary, high-payoff research that bridges the gap between fundamental discoveries and military use. The initial DARPA Grand Challenge in 2004 created a spurt of development in technologies needed to create the first fully autonomous ground vehicles capable of completing a substantial off-road course within a limited time. In 2004, no vehicle completed the course.

In 2005, Sebastian Thron, former director of Stanford's AI laboratories and co-creator of Google Street View, lead a team which created a robotic vehicle (Stanley) which won the DARPA Grand Challenge and the $2M prize. In 2008, Thron went to work at Google full-time.

Human error is involved in 94% of all vehicular accidents in the U.S. As a result of these accidents, every year approximately 32,000 to 33,000 thousand people are killed on the roads. Worldwide, the numbers are even more stunning. Approximately 1.2 million people are killed in traffic accidents worldwide annually. In fact, traffic accidents are the leading cause of death for people between the ages of 4 and 34, being more dangerous to young people than cancer or gun violence.

During the last 13 years of military operations in Iraq and Afghanistan, one of the leading causes of death for U.S. soldiers were improvised explosive devises (IEDs) targeting vehicles. Removing humans from vehicles can potentially reduce operational risk and lower casualties on the battlefield. Autonomous vehicles is a leading science and technology imitative within the Army.

Driverless cars can potentially solve these safety issues, and reduce fatalities on the roadways and the battlefield.

Competitors

Five companies competing with Alphabet in the autonomous vehicle arena include:

1. Tesla: Elon Musk, chairman and CEO of Tesla, told Financial Times in September that cars capable of taking over 90 percent of the driving from someone behind the wheel will be road-ready within three years. "It's incredibly hard to get the last few percent."

2. Nissan: Nissan leads the pack when it comes to its commitment to self-driving cars. The company recently announced it would offer them by 2020.

3. General Motors (GM): GM is working on autonomous features as part of an option package called Super Cruise. It lets a driver take his hands off the wheel at highway speeds and avoids colliding with other vehicles by combining adaptive cruise control and lane centering by employing radar, GPS and infrared optical cameras.

4. Ford: The founder of the Ford Driverless Car initiative, James McBride, recently stated in at article that, "Ford hopes to bring forth a Level 4 autonomous car. One that relies on no driver input, even in emergencies."[1] Ford recently acquired a permit to begin operating a driverless car on public streets as part of the California Autonomous Vehicle Testing Program. They are rolling out a small fleet of 2016 Ford Fusions to begin testing in Silicon Valley and San Francisco.

---

[1] http://www.latimes.com/business/autos/la-fi-hy-ford-driverless-car-to-hit-california-roads-20151215-story.html

5. Apple: Apple projects a 2019 ship-date for its secret electric car project, code-name Titan. Apple is increasingly "committed to entering the car market at a time when many believe the industry faces disruption."[2] The question is why is Apple doubling down on delivering an electric car rather than a driverless one? Part of the reason could be attributed to the appearance of being competitive, as opposed to those companies currently exploring autonomous vehicle technologies. Also, the cost of building a driverless car is much higher than the cost of building an electric one, along with the risk involved from autonomous vehicle emerging technology. Apple views their strategy as one where the company can introduce a car fully integrated with its existing operating systems before eventually changing to a driverless model. However, the company is keeping secrecy with regard to this project.

Legislation and Regulation[3]

Legislation, passed in four U.S. states and Washington, D.C., allow driverless cars. The state of Nevada passed a law on June 29, 2011 permitting the operation of autonomous cars. The Nevada Department of Motor Vehicles (NDMV) issued the first license for an autonomous car in May, 2012 to a Toyota Prius modified with Google's experimental driverless technology. A month prior, Florida became the second state to allow testing of autonomous cars on public roads. California became the third when Governor Jerry Brown sign the bill into law at Google's Headquarters in Mountain View, California. In December 2013, Michigan became the fourth state to allow testing of driverless cars on public roads.

Currently, there are two federal legislation bills under consideration. The first is House of Representatives (HR) Bill No. 22, FAST (Federal-Aid Highways and Highway Safety Construction Programs) ACT, which was introduced in December 2015 to the House Ways and Means Committee. The bill authorizes appropriations out of the Highway Trust Fund (HTF), except for mass transit appropriations, during fiscal years (FY) 2016-2021 for Intelligent Transportation Systems (ITS) programs.[4]

Section 12001 of the FAST ACT directs U.S. Department of Transportation (DOT) to use at least 50% of program funds to make competitive innovative grants to, and enter into cooperative agreements and contracts with, states, other federal agencies, local governments, metropolitan planning organizations, institutions of higher education, private sector, and nonprofit organizations to carry out demonstration programs to accelerate the deployment and adoption of transportation research activities. Section 12002 directs DOT to establish a competitive grant program to accelerate the deployment of the Intelligent Transportation System (ITS) program and ITS-enabled operational strategies to enhance mobility of people and goods on the surface transportation system.

HR Bill No. 3876, Autonomous Vehicle Privacy Protection Act of 2015, was introduced in November 2015 and is currently under review by House Transportation and Infrastructure Committee. The bill directs the U.S. Comptroller General to make available to the public a report that assesses the organizational readiness of the DOT to address vehicle technology challenges, including consumer privacy protections.[5]

In May 2014, Google presented their concept of autonomous vehicle technology, and unveiled a fully functioning prototype in December 2014. The company is currently testing their vehicles near the San Francisco Bay area, and it plans to make these cars available to the public in 2020. Figure 1 shows the current regulatory blanket across the U.S. and highlights the states with Google offices. This will help visualize the Corporate Problem which is addressed in the next section.

---

[2] http://www.theatlantic.com/technology/archive/2015/09/why-would-apple-make-an-electric-car-not-a-driverless-one/406645/

[3] https://en.wikipedia.org/wiki/Google_self-driving_car

[4] https://www.congress.gov/bill/114th-congress/house-bill/22

[5] https://www.congress.gov/bill/114th-congress/house-bill/3876/text?resultIndex=1

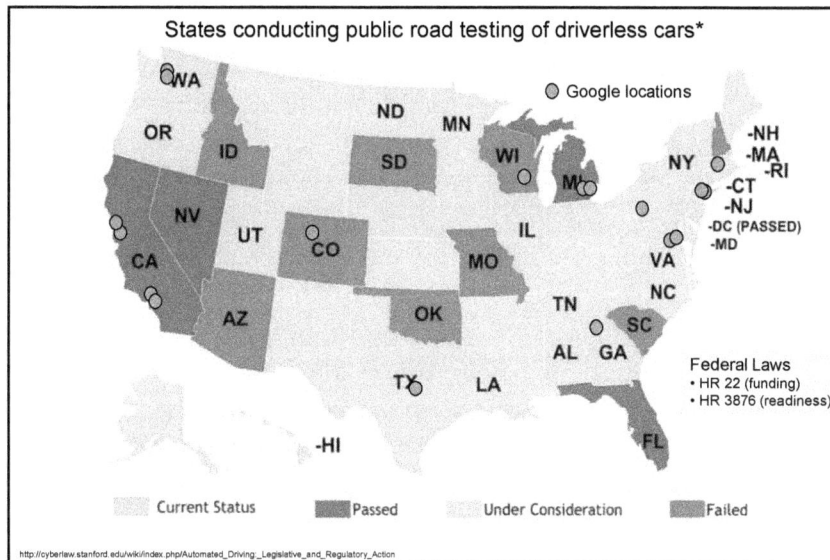

Figure 1. Current legislative landscape and Google locations.

Corporate Problem

For this case study, Google wants to expand their market research and testing locations outside their Mountain View, California and Austin, Texas testing centers. Google's California location tests completely autonomous vehicles – cars with no steering wheel and which cannot exceed 25 mph. Austin tests autonomous vehicles requiring a combination of gas and brake pedals, and a steering wheel. The corporate problem we are trying to solve is "*Which city should Google expand driverless cars into next?*"

Decision Criteria and Metrics

With nineteen locations throughout the U.S., Google wants to expand their market research and development in cities where its corporate offices are currently located. They are also considering markets with a population greater than 2 million residents[6], but not larger than 6 million residents. The reason to focus on limited population numbers, or density, is to preserve passenger safety, as these autonomous vehicles are progressively introduced into the roadways for testing. Additionally, the narrow focus on metro populations is to generate a list of candidates not exhibiting outlier behavior in accidents and roadway complexity.

The corporate decision criteria for this case study is as follows:

1. Minimize Traffic Accidents.
2. Maximize Number of Passengers.
3. Maximize Non-Passenger Utilization.
4. Maximize Public Relations.

<u>Minimize Traffic Accidents.</u> This criteria is defined as, minimize the number and severity of traffic accidents involving Google cars.

---

[6] Austin, Texas has a population just shy of 2 million, or 1.9 million.

In February, a Google self-driving car brushed against a bus. This is the first accident, in over one million miles driven, where the autonomous car was at fault. A Lexus RX 450h collided with a bus in Mountain View, CA. No one was injured as a result of the accident. The crash happened when the robotic SUV maneuvered toward the center lane to make a right turn around some sand bags -- both the vehicle and its test driver incorrectly assumed that a bus approaching from behind would slow or stop to let the car through. The Lexus impacted the side of the bus at low speed, damaging its front fender, wheel and sensor in the process.

<u>Maximize the number of Passengers</u>. Autonomous technology must provide alternatives to congested transportation infrastructure in cities.

<u>Maximize Non-Passenger Utilization</u>. Once the technology evolves into a more synchronized system of systems, the mature programs can further develop into other areas of corollary market place. Take, for example, Amazon's initiative to deliver packages by automated drones.[7] The speed of development in aerial drone technology is driven by consumer behavior; the idea of ordering something online and have it delivered rapidly to your door.

<u>Maximize Public Relations.</u> No company can undertake such a venture to revolutionize our way of life without the public support. In October, 2015 Tallinn University of Technology, in Estonia, asked their students to submit projects within their Techno-Psychology student review about "driverless cars-problems, benefits, and effects."[8] The study aimed to look at the psychological view of this evolution of new technology from the students' perspective.[9] The biggest concern amongst majority of the students was safety, but the psychological effects ranged from price, operating software issues, and more importantly, loss of jobs from the transportation industry along with the added investment in infrastructure improvements.

Figure 2 summarizes the Corporate Problem and Objectives.

Problem: Which city to expand Google Driverless car into next?	
Corporate Objectives	**Definitions**
Minimize Traffic Accidents	Minimize the number and severity of traffic accidents involving Google driverless cars.
Maximize Number of Passengers	Maximize the number of passengers driven.
Maximize Non-Passenger Utilization	Maximize the number of packages delivered.
Maximize Public Relations	Maximize good word of mouth and media coverage.

Figure 2. Corporate Problem and Objectives.

Figure 3 describes our decision criteria weights.

---

[7] https://www.yahoo.com/tech/exclusive-amazon-reveals-details-about-1343951725436982.html
[8] Driverless cars-problems, benefits, and effects. 15 October 2015, Techno-Psychology journal, Tallinn University of Technology.
[9] There is no reported data sets in this study, so it is uncertain whether the 63 project submissions are based on any quantitative measure, or are purely qualitative. The submissions are adequate to get an idea on perceptions towards driverless vehicles.

Our objective weights are provided, ranked in descending order of importance. The decision criteria weights are also shown. Note that "lowest accident rate" accounts for half of the other remaining attributes. The company considers safety as very significant, and divides traffic density and cost of accidents (severity) evenly at 25% each. For example, traffic density equals 0.4 x .25 = 0.10 or 10%. Similar calculations are presented for the remaining attributes with the corresponding resulting weights.

The number of passengers, non-passenger utilization, and public relations are maximizing functions highlighting the importance of the highest expected offset from public transportation, value and weight of potential cargo being transported by autonomous vehicles, as well as the public perception of this technology regarding environmental effects and user-friendly alternate mode of conveyance.

Objectives	Objective Weight	Decision Criteria (DC)	DC Weight	Resulting Weight
Minimize Traffic Accidents	40%	Traffic density	25%	10%
		Lowest accident rate	50%	20%
		Lowest accident severity	25%	10%
Maximize Number of Passengers	30%	Highest expected offset from public transportation.	40%	12%
		Population density.	30%	9%
		Parking availability.	30%	9%
Maximize Non-passenger Utilization	20%	Value of parcels.	60%	12%
		Weight of parcels.	40%	8%
Maximize Public Relations	10%	Environmental perception.	40%	4%
		Early adopter inclination.	60%	6%

Figure 3. Decision Criteria Weights.

Figure 4 describes the decision criteria used and quantifies each of the metrics based on our research data.

Corporate Objectives	Decision Criteria	Metric
Minimize Traffic Accidents	Traffic density (Cost of congestion and time of delay)	• Hours of delay per commuter (Ref.1) • Less is better (Min/Score)
	Lowest accident rate (Fewest number of accidents per mile)	• Number of injuries/Metro population (Ref.2) • Less is better (Min/Score)
	Lowest accident severity (Fewest fatalities and lowest cost per accident)	• Total cost of accidents/Metro population (Ref 3) • Less is better (Min/Score)
Maximize Number of Passengers	Highest expected offset from public transportation. (Percent of commuters of each transportation type.)	• Number of trips x (Percent of motor bus + light rail + commuter rail) (Ref.4) • More is better (Score/Max)
	Population density	• Persons per square mile (sq./mi) (Ref.5) • More is better (Score/Max)
	Parking availability (Ratio of available parking vs. commuters.)	• Parking garages and lots per 1000 commuter vehicles (Ref.6) • Less is better (Min/Score)
Maximize Non-passenger Utilization	Value of parcels. (Maximize value of packages delivered.)	• Metropolitan area Table 1 (Ref.7) • More is better (Score/Max)
	Weight of parcels. (Maximize weight delivered.)	• Metropolitan area Table 1 (Ref.8) • More is better (Score/Max)
Maximize Public Relations	Environmental perception. (City's preference toward environmentally friendly technology.)	• SME Voting (Ref.9) • More is better (Score/Max)
	Early adopter inclination. (Willingness to adopt emerging technologies.)	• SME Voting (Ref.10) • More is better (Score/Max)

Figure 4. Decision Criteria Metrics.

Alternatives

In order to scope the analysis, initial screening criteria were developed to assess the potential city alternatives from the top 50 U.S. cities, based on population size. As a result, of senior decision maker input initial screening criteria included the following:

1) The city must have a Google branch – this left 19 cities remaining,
2) The city must be east of the Mississippi River – this left 10 cities remaining,
3) The population density of the alternatives must be less than the current project cities – this left 6 cities remaining,
4) The alternative must have a population great than 1 million people – this left 3 cities remaining.

Using this screening criteria filtered down the initial list to 3 possible alternatives:

- Atlanta, Ga.
- Birmingham/Detroit, MI.
- Pittsburgh, PA.

Analysis Methodology

Constraints, Limitation, and Assumptions

The following guidelines and restrictions were helpful to frame the scope and context of the business problem to produce timely, relevant and actionable results for the decision makers:

Constraints: A restriction imposed by the study sponsor that limits the study team's options in conducting the study.

- Analysis must be completed by May 2, 2016.

Limitations: Circumstances that limit the study team's ability to fully meet the study objective or fully investigate the study issues.

- Data availability (the study must use readily/publically sourced datasets due to time available).

Assumptions: Taken as true in the absence of facts, often to accommodate a limitation.

- Fleet size and cost is constant for all cities (fleet cost is removed from the location analysis).
- Government regulations permit driverless cars to operate.
- Open source data sufficient (applicable and accurate) for analysis.

Raw Data Scores

Use of Government transportation and population statistics pertaining to the study locations resulted in the following table of raw and normalized scores for the three candidate cities, as well as the representative locations associated with the minimum and maximum values for each criteria. For the two subjective attribute categories, the study team polled responses from the Google Market Research Division, using a linear Likert scale of 1 to 9 (worst to best) in the categories for Environmental Perception and early Adopter Inclination. The minimum and maximum values were used to generate the normalized scale, according to the following formulas:

For minimizing goals: normalized score is the representative minimum ÷ alternative score.
For maximizing goals: normalized score is the alternative score ÷ representative maximum.

	Alt 1	Alt 2	Alt 3	Minimum	Maximum
	Atlanta, GA	Detroit, MI	Pittsburgh, PA	Raleigh	Washington DC
Traffic Density	52	52	39	34	82
Normalized Score	0.6538	0.6538	0.8718		
	Atlanta, GA	Detroit, MI	Pittsburgh, PA	Raleigh	Washington DC
Lowest Accident Rate	0.0138	0.0083	0.0082	0.0023	0.0190
Normalized Score	0.1704	0.2841	0.2873		
	Atlanta, GA	Detroit, MI	Pittsburgh, PA	Denver	Nashville
Lowest Accident Severity	0.0024	0.0015	0.0018	0.0007	0.0035
Normalized Score	0.2751	0.4318	0.3713		
	Atlanta, GA	Detroit, MI	Pittsburgh, PA	Oklahoma City	New York
Percent of Commuters	65581.78	40383.28	62647.13	2847.94	1470366.07
Normalized Score	0.0446	0.0275	0.0426		
	Atlanta, GA	Detroit, MI	Pittsburgh, PA	Atlanta	Los Angeles
Population Density	1706.90	2792.50	1915.50	1706.90	6999.30
Normalized Score	0.2439	0.3990	0.2737		
	Atlanta, GA	Detroit, MI	Pittsburgh, PA	Oklahoma City	Pittsburgh
Parking Availability	1.38	0.49	4.19	0.07	4.19
Normalized Score	0.0507	0.1429	0.0167		
	Atlanta, GA	Detroit, MI	Pittsburgh, PA	Washington DC	Los Angeles
Value of Parcels	30622	16692	11340	365	154934
Normalized Score	0.1976	0.1077	0.0732		
	Atlanta, GA	Detroit, MI	Pittsburgh, PA	Washington DC	Los Angeles
Weight of Parcels	1069	385	206	6	3545
Normalized Score	0.3016	0.1086	0.0581		
	Atlanta, GA	Detroit, MI	Pittsburgh, PA	Reject Eco Tech	Prefer Eco Tech
Environmental Perception	6	4	7	1	9
Normalized Score	0.6667	0.4444	0.7778		
	Atlanta, GA	Detroit, MI	Pittsburgh, PA	Unwilling to Adopt	Willing to Adopt
Early Adopter Inclination	7	4	6	1	9
Normalized Score	0.7778	0.4444	0.6667		

Figure 5. Raw and Normalized Scores.

Simple Additive Weighing (SAW) Method

The prevalent and straightforward SAW method applies the attribute weights as a coefficient to each alternative's normalized score, and sums these results across all attributes for each alternative for a resultant total. This straightforward sum of products of the weights × normalized values results in the alternative scores for each city, provided below:

	Global Weights											
	0.1	0.2	0.1	0.12	0.09	0.09	0.12	0.08	0.04	0.06	Final Score	
	Traffic Density	Lowest Accident Rate	Lowest Accident Severity	Percent of Commuters	Population Density	Parking Availability	Value of Parcels	Weight of Parcels	Environmental Perception	Early Adopter Inclination		
Atlanta, GA	0.6538	0.1704	0.2751	0.0446	0.2439	0.0507	0.1976	0.3016	0.6667	0.7778	0.2800	
Detroit, MI	0.6538	0.2841	0.4318	0.0275	0.3990	0.1429	0.1077	0.1086	0.4444	0.4444	0.2835	
Pittsburgh, PA	0.8718	0.2873	0.3713	0.0426	0.2737	0.0167	0.0732	0.0581	0.7778	0.6667	0.2976	1

Figure 6. Simple Additive Weighting Scores for Each Alternative.

Results

The results of the SAW method indicate that Pittsburgh is the top alternative, based on the decision-maker's weightings and city attributes. Detroit was the second best scoring alternative, and Atlanta a very close third.

The study team investigated the possible impact of recent news events on these results, namely the minor collision[10] of a Google Car with a city bus in Mountain View, CA, and the Flint (Detroit suburb) water crisis fallout[11]. The collision could affect Early Adopter Inclination in areas like Atlanta that previously had a high adopter value, and the shrinking population of Detroit could affect the Environmental Perception value. At this time, neither event resulted in a significant change in preference or scoring, but the study team will continue to monitor public perception and sentiment in the markets for both of these events.

The study team's recommendation is to pursue Google Car program expansion into the top alternative: Pittsburgh, PA. We recommend a staged progression of expansion if a second city is considered. Specifically, the second choice by SAW results is Detroit, MI, but it may be prudent to both wait for the results in Pittsburgh, as well as continue to monitor the environmental impacts in the Detroit area and the early adopter inclination in Atlanta to determine if recent news becomes an accelerating trend which may warrant adjustment of further expansion into Atlanta rather than Detroit.

Sensitivity Analysis

We conducted a sensitivity of the model to better inform the decision on how volatile the recommend alternative may be based on the objectives and decision criteria. This shows the decision maker changes to the recommended alternative due to re-weighting of objectives and criteria, as well as provide some insight to what attributes are the most influential and which ones are not.

The methodology used in conducting our sensitivity analysis was to analyze each attribute weight individually. We used as a baseline, the weights provided by the decision maker and then changed the weight (increasing and decreasing) of one attribute to identify the threshold point where the recommended alternative would change. Once an iteratively adjusted weighting resulted in a change of the outcome, the changed weight was recorded (for both lower bound and upper bound where applicable) for each attribute, establishing sensitivity limits for the current attribute weights. Prior to each new set of iterations, we reset the model to the baseline weighting. This allows us and the decision maker to see how volatile the recommendation is based on if we changed that one attribute's weight.

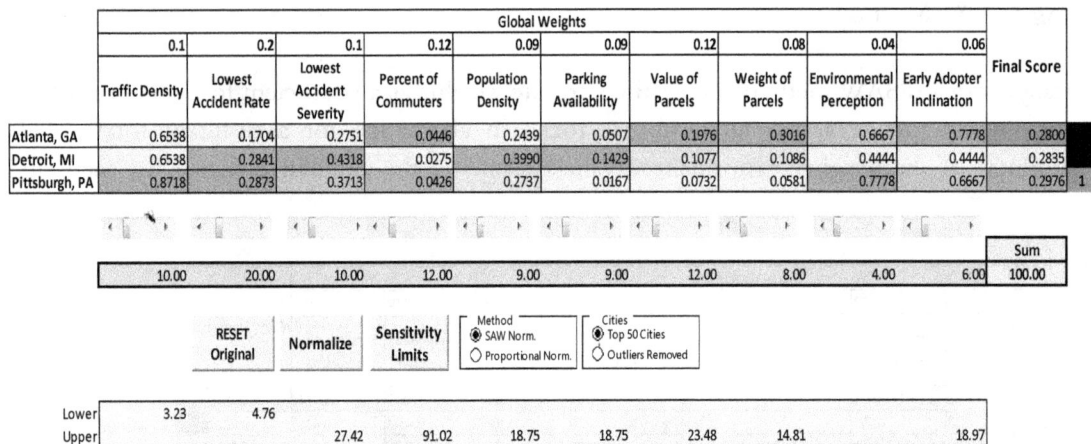

	Global Weights										
	0.1	0.2	0.1	0.12	0.09	0.09	0.12	0.08	0.04	0.06	Final Score
	Traffic Density	Lowest Accident Rate	Lowest Accident Severity	Percent of Commuters	Population Density	Parking Availability	Value of Parcels	Weight of Parcels	Environmental Perception	Early Adopter Inclination	
Atlanta, GA	0.6538	0.1704	0.2751	0.0446	0.2439	0.0507	0.1976	0.3016	0.6667	0.7778	0.2800
Detroit, MI	0.6538	0.2841	0.4318	0.0275	0.3990	0.1429	0.1077	0.1086	0.4444	0.4444	0.2835
Pittsburgh, PA	0.8718	0.2873	0.3713	0.0426	0.2737	0.0167	0.0732	0.0581	0.7778	0.6667	0.2976	1

	Traffic Density	Lowest Accident Rate	Lowest Accident Severity	Percent of Commuters	Population Density	Parking Availability	Value of Parcels	Weight of Parcels	Environmental Perception	Early Adopter Inclination	Sum
	10.00	20.00	10.00	12.00	9.00	9.00	12.00	8.00	4.00	6.00	100.00

RESET Original	Normalize	Sensitivity Limits	Method	Cities
			◉ SAW Norm. ○ Proportional Norm.	◉ Top 50 Cities ○ Outliers Removed

	Traffic Density	Lowest Accident Rate	Lowest Accident Severity	Percent of Commuters	Population Density	Parking Availability	Value of Parcels	Weight of Parcels	Environmental Perception	Early Adopter Inclination
Lower	3.23	4.76								
Upper			27.42	91.02	18.75	18.75	23.48	14.81		18.97

Figure 7. Sensitivity Analysis by Iterative Adjustment.

---

[10] Google Self-Driving Car Crash. CNET Road Show news available at http://www.cnet.com/roadshow/news/googles-chris-urmson-explain-self-driving-car-crash/

[11] Fastest Shrinking Cities. USA Today available at http://www.usatoday.com/story/money/business/2014/04/19/24-7-wallst-shrinking-cities/7871157/

Additionally, we investigated the use of an alternative normalization technique (proportional weighting) as well as removal of outliers in the normalization minimum and maximum representative city sets. The alternative normalization technique of proportional weighting is achieved as a linear scoring value between 0 and 1, where cities equal to the minimum value are scored as 0, cities at the maximum level are scored as 1, and all others scores as a linear proportion of the distance between these limits (based on a maximized attribute). This alternative technique does result in a change in outcome, indicating a choice of Detroit, rather than Pittsburgh. However, this method is a departure from the SAW method, and the data did not contain enough inherent natural skewing to warrant this alternative approach. When investigating the list of minimum and maximum city values, New York stood out as an outlier (by a clear order of magnitude difference between it and the next highest city in terms of percent of commuters). We removed New York (replacing it with #2: Los Angeles) to determine the effects. However, no change in outcome resulted from this outlier removal versus the original inclusion.

After conducting the sensitivity analysis of each attributes' weight, several insights were identified. Out of the ten attributes, only one attribute, environmental perception, had no threshold point. That is, no matter how high or low the weight for environment perception is weighted, the attribute does not have an impact on the recommended alternative. This is due to the fact that the recommended alternative it has the highest score for environmental perception so the ranking will not change as you increase the weight. The recommended alternative does not change when you decrease the attribute's weight because the original weighting of the environmental perception is already low (global weight of 4%). Basically, environmental perception currently has no impact on the recommendation.

Out of the remaining nine attributes, only two show significant influence over the recommended alternative. Both traffic density and weight of parcels provide a different recommended alternative if the weight is changed by less than ten percent. In the case for traffic density, the recommended alternative changes from Pittsburgh to Detroit when the global weight changes from ten percent to three percent. Though this attribute is volatile, the likelihood that the importance of traffic density to decrease, being that it feeds the objective of minimizing traffic accidents, is very low. For weight of parcels, the recommended alternative changes from Pittsburgh to Atlanta when the weight increases from eight percent to 15 percent. Again, looking at the likelihood of the increasing the importance of weight of parcels is low because the objective of maximizing non-passenger utilization would need to be more important than maximizing passenger utilization. With respect to the recommended alternative of Pittsburgh being the next location for the Google Car project, the solution is not sensitive due to attribute weighting.

References

1. Hours of Delay per commuter - Table 5-5: Highway Congestion in 50 Largest Urban Areas: 2014, Bureau of Transportation Statistics.
2. Number of Injuries / Metro Population - Table A.1 Cambridge Systematics Fatalities and Injuries by City; Table 4-3 Transit Ridership in 50 Largest Urban Areas 2013, BTS.
3. Total Cost of Accidents / Metro Population - Table A.1 Cambridge Systematics Fatalities and Injuries by City; Table 4-3 Transit Ridership in 50 Largest Urban Areas 2013, BTS.
4. Number of Trips * (Percent of Motor Bus + Light Rail + Commuter Rail); Table 4-3 Transit Ridership in 50 Largest Urban Areas 2013, BTS.
5. Persons per square mile - 2010 US Census Data.
6. Parking Garages and Lots per 1000 Commuter Vehicles - NerdWallet, 2016.
7. Value of parcels - Metropolitan Area Table 1, 2007 Commodity Flow Survey, BTS.
8. Weight of parcels - Metropolitan Area Table 1, 2007 Commodity Flow Survey, BTS.
9. Environmental perception – SME voting. Pittsburgh: trying to clean up city; Atlanta might get Porsche plant - very tech forward; Detroit has several traditional auto manufacturers.
10. Early adopter Inclination – SME voting. Pittsburgh converting to tech/banking from steel industry; Atlanta is tech hub; Detroit tech revolves around existing auto manufacturer.
11. Google Self-Driving Car Crash. CNET Road Show news available at http://www.cnet.com/roadshow/news/googles-chris-urmson-explain-self-driving-car-crash/
12. Fastest Shrinking Cities. USA Today available at http://www.usatoday.com/story/money/business/2014/04/19/24-7-wallst-shrinking-cities/7871157/

ABOUT THE AUTHORS

Frank A. Tillman, PhD, PE, has a varied career of over thirty years in academia, consulting, and real estate development. He served as department head at Kansas State University for more than twenty years, where he published over fifty professional articles and four books. He has also authored several books for professionals identifying the approaches that work best for solving problems and offering practicable solutions.

Deandra T. Cassone, PhD, PMP, serves as an associate professor in the Industrial and Manufacturing Systems Engineering program at Kansas State University and has been in management at a Fortune 100 company. Her career of over twenty-five years includes consulting, technical, and management roles and has published two books. With an interest in building structured decision making models, she has been awarded numerous business process patents.

Together they have authored *A Professional's Guide to Decision Science and Problem Solving, The Science of Common Sense: Best Practical Decision Science Methods* and *Evaluating Products and Projects to Meet Corporate Objectives.*

Dedication
Frank A. Tillman, PhD, PE
July 22, 1937 – February 26, 2017

Frank was born July 22, 1937 in Linn, Missouri. The unfortunate early passing of his father started him working at the age of nine. This work ethic carried throughout his life. Frank was an athlete through high school and went to college at Lincoln University on a basketball scholarship. He soon realized that academia was his passion. Frank was married to Barbara Langendoerfer and they shared 58 years together at the time of his death. Working full-time to support his family and going to school full-time he earned a Bachelors and Master's Degree in Industrial Engineering from the University of Missouri. He worked at Standard Oil of Ohio and attended Case Institute working on his Ph.D. in Operations Research. He was awarded a Ford Foundation grant to finish his Ph.D. at the University of Iowa in Industrial Engineering.

After graduating, he moved his family to Manhattan, Kansas and took a position as a Professor at Kansas State University. A year later, at 29, he became Head of the Department of Industrial Engineering. Frank loved academics. He mentored many students throughout his career that have become very successful and kept in touch with him over time. As Professor and Department Head, he was instrumental in the approval of the engineering PhD program, he was a founder of the KSU Chapter of Tau Beta Pi, and was involved in Alpha Pi Mu, ABET accreditation, was an Institute of Industrial Engineering fellow, wrote fifty-four papers and two books during his time on the faculty and was awarded emeritus status upon his departure from the university. Frank was also inducted into the KSU Engineering Hall of Fame. Frank began his real estate development career during this time as well, developing a number of housing communities in Manhattan, Kansas. In 1972, he received a Presidential appointment to U.S. President Nixon's Price Commission and moved his family to Washington DC for a short time.

He began consulting businesses which drew him from academia to the business world as his primary career. He operated two successful consulting companies with many contracts with government agencies and Fortune 500 companies. He spent the next twenty years managing these firms with offices in Manhattan and Washington DC. Frank also continued his real estate activities with commercial and residential real estate. In Frank's later years, he published four books and four eBooks documenting his approach to problem solving and applying theory to practical solutions.

Frank was very active in the community. He served two terms on the USD 383 School Board, served on multiple advisory councils and coached numerous basketball, softball and baseball teams. His Youth Activities Foundation supported numerous sports teams in Manhattan and Kansas City. Frank and Barbara additionally support a scholarship fund for Industrial Engineering students and were Seaton Founders for the College of Engineering. One of his most treasured activities was coffee in the morning with KSU faculty and community members.

Of all of his abilities and passions, his family was always first and foremost to him. He was a man that cared for his family deeply and provided for them unceasingly. He was very involved in their lives and was happy to take them on family vacations to Disney World, ski trips, the Lake of the Ozarks and helping his kids and grandkids through college.

Frank touched many lives in his time here on earth, including students, athletes, business community members, faculty and friends. He always saw potential in people who were discouraged in engineering. He endlessly recruited for the Industrial Engineering Department. He always had an opinion and was happy to discuss it with you.

For me personally, he was my father, my mentor and my friend and he is deeply missed.

Deandra Cassone, PhD, PMP